How to Learn Through Conflict

A Handbook for Leaders in Local Churches

Colin Patterson

Lay Development Officer, Diocese of Durham

GROVE BOOKS LIMITED

RIDLEY HALL RD CAMBRIDGE CB3 9HU

Contents

Acknowledgments

I am indebted to following people:

- Those who have allowed me to use case histories of conflict in their churches on pages 11, 15–16 and 21. The stories given are all true but for obvious reasons I have kept them anonymous.
- Carolyn Schrock-Shenk, for several pithy phrases.
- Gavin Wakefield, for encouraging an inexperienced author.
- Alastair McKay, Director of Bridge Builders, whose advice and example have been hugely influential.

The Cover Illustration is by Campbell Patterson (after M C Escher)

First Impression December 2003
ISSN 0144-171X
ISBN 1 85174 547 5

Introduction 1

Why a booklet on conflict? Well, to state the obvious, the church has plenty of conflict on its hands.

You can light the blue touch paper in local churches simply by holding a committee meeting, or inviting the wrong person to run a cake stall, or changing a well-established custom in worship. Worse, newspaper reporters can usually depend on Revd Rentaquote to carp about something.

But conflict is more than just an in-house issue for the church. It is a *world* issue—especially so since 11th September 2001—and the church is called to make a difference in the world. What might that mean at a time when traditional assumptions about war and security have been shaken? I think that offering ethical advice about just wars is not enough. Nor is simply comforting those in distress. The church ought to be an *example,* a community that models constructive responses to conflict.

And here we become uncomfortable. We are embarrassed when conflict exposes our true mettle as a believing community, if our Christianity is seen to be little more than a hobby. My impression is that many Christians tend to sweep conflict under the carpet. Then hostility either simmers in the background or explodes, neither of which is constructive. If the gospel is about transforming soured relationships then surely church leaders should be able to take active steps towards that goal rather than settling for damage limitation.

In practice, how could we do better? I suspect that many share with me a sense of being ill-equipped. I was trained how to handle conflicting *ideas,* but not how to handle conflicting *people.* And skilful face-to-face communication does not come naturally to me. So I have undertaken training in handling conflict, and it has affected the whole course of my ministry. I now spend a significant part of my time running training workshops myself, as well as offering help to Christians who are bogged down in disagreement.

This handbook is based on tested practice—my own and other people's—so it is not abstract theory. The text is deliberately interspersed with exercises. Some you can do by yourself; some are best done in a group such as a church council or leadership team. I hope that what you find here will give you fresh confidence that, whatever the conflict, God is with you there in the thick of it.

2 Is It Possible?

Christians do not, on the whole, behave as if they believe conflict can be a medium for learning.

Endure conflict? Yes, perhaps. But walk towards it as a pathway to maturity? 'You can*not* be serious!' Yet it does happen. In preparation for writing this booklet, I appealed through various networks for first hand stories of learning through conflict. I received a number of moving responses (three of which are shown opposite). Individuals and groups testified that, having faced conflict, they are stronger, and the whole experience has been spiritually formative. I learned a lot simply by listening to what they told me. But, further, they frequently said that sharing their stories with me had helped them too, by allowing them a further chance to process what they had learned in the crucible of conflict.

> I am using the word conflict to cover any case where having different goals leads to tension—anything from a mild difference of opinion to entrenched opposition.

It is essential, then, that if people are to learn anything through conflict, they must acknowledge the experience for what it is, and be willing to talk about it. Here we meet a problem. No one will open up on the subject unless he or she is persuaded that conflict is not in itself bad, that there is no necessary shame in being caught up in it. But many Christians do feel that if only we loved one another then conflict would simply never arise. So when it happens, it becomes unmentionable.

Why so? Beings who are free to choose are bound to come into conflict at times. But as redeemed servants of Christ we are not bound to a cycle of bitterness, recrimination and revenge. Discipleship succeeds or fails in the way we *respond* to conflict. Will we build up or tear down? Will we be the Holy Spirit's pupils?

To Think About

- Do a quick bit of word association: what other words or phrases come straight to mind when you hear the word *conflict*? Jot them down.
- Look at what you have written. How much of it has a destructive feel? How many of the words / phrases imply something constructive?

- Think of a recent experience of conflict that you have been through (it need not be a very severe one). Have you ever stopped to ask yourself, 'What did I *learn* from all that?'
- Read the three stories below. What do they have in common?

Three Experiences of Conflict

It was a row about discipline versus forgiveness. A church member was released from prison after serving a sentence for a sexual offence. The congregation divided between those who felt he was wrongly convicted, and those who were deeply critical. At the bishop's direction, the vicar declined to give him communion until he had publicly expressed regret. Further polarization! Two of us were asked to mediate between the vicar and unhappy members. During three sessions, attended by the majority of the congregation, we created a forum in which people could express their views and listen carefully to those they disagreed with. It gave the vicar a chance to explain the action that had been taken. More light than heat was generated and it was the beginning of healing and fresh spiritual growth.

It was a very steep learning curve! No manual tells you what to do when the church building burns down. Some wanted the old one rebuilt. The insurance wouldn't cover that. English Heritage opposed plans for a new building. The church council pulled together unanimously but some in the congregation and local community had reservations. They became very vocal, feeling sidelined by the council's solidarity. But in the end the design of the new building had a unifying effect. The architect carefully made the site's potential clear, talked to the congregation, and ensured there were many contributors to the final plan. A Christian lawyer acted as a go-between with the fiercest opponents. He got to the root of their objections, and some of their concerns were incorporated into the design. The new plan was well supported. People with the right skills to move it on just kept popping up.

We inherited a situation with resentment between morning and evening congregations and a church council that had a reputation for crucifying clergy. Grudges going back 15–20 years kept coming up. At first it was like clearing mines. We tried to be as even-handed as possible, and spent time visiting and letting people have their say. It took longer than we expected to establish trust, but patient work with the church council clarified the issues and made it possible to start solving some problems. We insisted that neither group could bully the other. In the latest round of changes in worship, there was a much more positive response. It taught us how important it is to allow plenty of discussion. Every option was looked at carefully and, once people felt listened to, they were prepared to move. I think the 'bullies' are learning that they can be heard without having to shout.

3 Learning from Scripture

Where do you begin in persuading Christians that conflict is not just an unseemly topic, best hushed up?

A useful starting place is to invite them to read the New Testament 'through conflict lenses,' to think themselves into the human drama on every page: the disputes caused by Jesus' teaching and behaviour; the tensions between Jewish and Gentile believers; the major councils called in the early church; the arguments between Paul and his opponents. It will be obvious that conflict is not an obscure or incidental theme. Indeed, a significant proportion of the New Testament was written specifically to respond to conflict, or anticipate it. Conclusion: we are all sinners, and conflict is normal and inevitable.

It may come as something of a relief to realize that the earliest churches—just like ours—experienced conflict within their fellowships. More specifically, in amongst the ordinary personal squabbles between individuals there was the threat of major rifts between groups with different cultural backgrounds. But it may also be sobering to discover that disunity is not treated with a mere shrug of the shoulders. It is seen as a scandalous denial of what it means for the church to be one body. The bottom line is that a disciple of Jesus is required to take action to restore damaged relationships.

To Do

Put together a *conflict Scripture collage:*

- Try to think of as many New Testament verses as you can, relevant to conflict within the church. Write each one out on a separate small card. Use bright red ink for the words that express emotions. (You could also do this as a group activity.)
- For the next few weeks, in your regular Bible reading, be alert for further conflict Scriptures and add them to your collection of cards.
- Paste the cards onto a backing sheet (add pictures or photos if you want) and hang your collage so that you can see it when you are praying for your church.

Try reading through the Gospel of Mark, with just this question in mind: *How did Jesus respond to conflict?*

Three New Testament Signposts

1 The Epistles Urge Active Peacemaking Within Congregations

I want to focus on two epistles in particular: Ephesians, because of its sublime vision of the church, and James because of its intense practicality.

Ephesians is built on Paul's prayerful concern (Eph 1.15–19a, 3.14–21) that Christians should live up to their calling (4.1). They are to be a new sort of community: the family of God (3.15), the body of Christ (1.23, 4.4 and 16) and the dwelling place of the Holy Spirit (2.22). God is concerned, says Paul, to destroy dividing walls of hostility (2.14), in particular between Jew and Gentile, and so bitterness, rage, anger and slander amongst Christians are actually grievous to the Spirit (4.30–31). Submission to one another is the way to honour Christ (5.21), and our hostility is to be directed towards the powers of darkness, not towards one another (6.11–12).

James faces his readers with the uncomfortable proposition that they should count it pure joy when they face trials (Jas 1.2). Christian maturity, he says, comes through perseverance (1.4), often in the face of opposition from those who are supposed to be on our side (4.1–3, 5.11). The wise Christian is the one who knows how to set aside selfish ambition and humbly submit to God who purifies our hearts (3.13–16, 4.7–10). Wisdom means being prepared to *wait* (5.7–10), slow to take offence and quick to *listen* (1.19), aware of the damage we can do by what we say (3.1–12). And God is willing to give us that sort of wisdom if we really want it (1.5–6).

Wisdom means being prepared to wait, slow to take offence and quick to listen

I have recently taken up a new hobby: polishing stones. You take a pile of rough pebbles and put them in a round drum with grit and water. Then a motor turns the drum for days and days until you get pretty, shiny stones. This is an attractive image of Christians facing conflict. We bang up against one another and in the process we get our rough edges knocked off. *But it is the wrong image*. It suggests something entirely passive, all the work being done by the motor. Paul and James, however, point to something much more active. The two letters we have just surveyed, in spite of their different tone, have matching centres. Paul: 'Make every effort to maintain the unity of the Spirit in the bond of peace' (Eph 4.2). James: 'Peacemakers who sow in peace raise a harvest of righteousness' (Jas 3.18). They echo Jesus' command to go and be reconciled when you know that another Christian has something against you (Matthew 5.23–24). If you know there is something not right between you, even if you feel in no way to blame, then you cannot simply let it rest—indeed it will be a hindrance to your worship.

2 Jesus Gave a 'Grievance Procedure' for Individuals to Follow

Matthew 18.15–17 takes us further. The most obvious implication is that if a fellow believer wrongs you, you should go and take it up with *that* person. Jesus indicates here that, if you seek an opportunity to be listened to in private, many grievances can be recognized and resolved without festering. Being realistic, some will not be thus resolved, often because the person you are rebuking does not accept your version of events. Hence Jesus' exhortation to pursue the matter further in the presence of one or two others who can give a more objective view. Only in the most difficult cases, after these other approaches have failed, should you report the matter to someone in authority in the church.

This teaching requires me (a) to *listen* when a grievance is raised, and (b) to *take the initiative* when aggrieved—or even as a third party. Literally, the text reads 'If your brother sins [against you], go reprove him…' but the bracketed words are not in the best manuscripts. So the command may well include 'Try to *mediate* when you are aware that others are out of sorts.'

3 The Apostles Mediated When Hostility Arose Between Different Groups

Acts 6.1–7 recounts a dispute between two groups of believers from different backgrounds. Widows from among the Greek-speaking community felt that they were being neglected in favour of Hebrew-speaking people during the distribution of aid. The conflict was resolved by the apostles taking specific action. First the grievance was acknowledged. Second, the apostles gave the whole congregation the responsibility for deciding whom they could trust to resolve the difficulty. Seven were chosen, to wide acclaim, and their names suggest that they belonged the Greek-speaking group. Note that because the apostles were willing to give power to those who felt sidelined, they re-established a climate of trust and there was growth in numbers.

Because the apostles were willing to give power to those who felt sidelined, they re-established a climate of trust

Acts 15.1–31 gives a detailed account of a Council called to deal with tension between Jewish and Gentile believers. The issue was whether Gentiles needed to be circumcised and obey the Law of Moses. Some Jews were demanding conformity. For them, it was about the terms for accepting Gentiles amongst God's people. The impressive thing about the Council is the time taken, ensuring that everyone's views were heard carefully. With widespread support (v 22) and a sense that the Holy Spirit had spoken (v 28) the apostles set out a way forward that laid no unnecessary burden on Gentile believers but nevertheless was sensitive to Jewish concerns.

From Head to Heart

It is important to open people's eyes to these strong New Testament themes. But that is not enough. What we learn has then to be moved from head to heart.

We all find it difficult to *apply* what we learn from the Bible. It is one thing to accept in a general sort of way that a Christian should make every effort to keep the unity of the Spirit in the bond of peace. It is quite another to be able to recognize a dividing wall of hostility and know what to do about it. Furthermore, old attitudes and patterns of behaviour often need *un*learning—and the more the subject matter touches on personal wounds the bigger the problem is. When you are immersed in conflict, your mind can tell you one thing ('I ought to forgive') while your emotions tell you another ('I feel too hurt'). You may defend yourself by invoking a string of rationalizations: 'I'm not angry'; 'It doesn't matter'; 'I know he wouldn't listen'; 'They'll never change'; 'I've already forgiven her, so the matter is closed.'

Having painted yourself into this sort of corner, the only way out is to *listen with an open heart*. Listen to your own feelings, which are the driving force behind your responses. Listen to the people who are upsetting you—you will not know their side of the story unless you deal with the dispute by direct communication. Listen to the inner witness of the Holy Spirit. The knowledge you need in these moments is not just Christian teaching but also a seeing of things as God sees them. You may discover that you are less reasonable than you like to think, and others are less selfish; behind what is happening, you may discern a spirit that can only be conquered by prayer and fasting. Such knowledge is painful to bear, like bright sunlight streaming into a darkened room, stabbing eyes and exposing nakedness. But when a new Spirit-given understanding dawns upon individuals, or even upon a whole group, conflict can be transformed (compare Acts 15.12).

Having painted yourself into this sort of corner, the only way out is to listen with an open heart

Let me be honest. I would rather help others to grow through facing conflict than do so myself! But I cannot teach others to do what I myself fail to model. Reluctantly and hesitatingly starting with myself, I have found that there are three questions I need to ask:

- How do I normally respond to conflict?
- How am I part of the problem?
- How can I be part of the solution?

I need to go on asking them, and I need to teach others to do the same.

4 Different Ways of Responding

Conflict usually drops on me unannounced, so I respond according to habit rather than plan.

Habits are personal things. Some of mine are good ones that I have deliberately adopted. Some of them I have just picked up by copying others or doing what seemed like a good idea at the time.

My habits may not be the same as yours. I get drained by conflict and find it harder and harder to make decisions. You may get energized by the tension and become more focused and determined. I become more task-oriented under pressure. (People sometimes ask me whether I have any idea what is going on around me.) You may focus more on other people when stress levels go up.

I have one-way vision. It is easy for me to see what *your* habits are yet I am not so aware of my own unless I choose to examine them. However, when I recognize what are my usual responses to conflict, it helps me to start increasing my repertoire. (Most of us in fact use a rather limited range.)

To Do

Examine yourself for a few minutes:

- Look at the four character sketches opposite. What 'colour' are you? (You may well be a mixture.)
- Now think back to some recent moment when you were in conflict with someone else. How did you respond?
  - — Did you back off (because you usually do)?
  - — Did you argue back strongly (because you usually do)?
  - — Did you have the control (of yourself or the situation) that you wanted?
  - — Have you fallen into a repeated pattern of behaviour with the person(s) concerned?

Questions like these can help to identify your house-style for responding to conflict. Now, everyone's style has strengths in some circumstances and weaknesses in others. But I find that I judge other people's unconstructive habits more severely than my own. For example, another person's difficulty with keeping to a timetable causes havoc, in my view, but my own reluctance to share my feelings is hardly something to get annoyed about.

Four Different People Responding to Conflict

Green I am the sort of person who likes to get things done. By giving a lead, I get others to follow, which stops them getting bogged down or caught up in squabbles. I love challenges—pressure gets me fired up. I have lots of ideas and look for new ways of doing things. My patience runs out with people who do not bother trying; I am told I should consult and listen more. The things that bring out the worst in me are getting no response, dull jobs, being insulted, and having responsibilities taken away from me.

Blue I am the sort of person who enjoys working out how things tick. By making careful plans, I protect us all from making mistakes. I can stick to a timetable but I tend to cave in when I am pushed to go too fast. For the sake of a project, I will set my own feelings aside. I back off fast when other people get emotional; I am told I am rather detached. The things that bring out the worst in me are others failing to follow through, not knowing how much time is needed, and being made to look foolish.

Red I am the sort of person who loves to be in a team with high standards. By working hard for worthwhile causes, I help us all to do well. I support and encourage others and expect the same in return. I will cooperate with a boss I respect, but challenge any cutting of corners. I believe we can learn from experience and do better next time. However, I brood a lot over difficulties; I am told I am rather defensive and perfectionist. The things that bring out the worst in me are criticism, being taken advantage of, and having everything dumped on my shoulders.

Yellow I am the sort of person who enjoys helping others to get on together. By being good-natured, I smooth things along and so prevent conflict. I am quite willing to revise my plans so as to preserve harmony. Other people's feelings matter to me and I am quick to forgive. I hate confrontation, and will agree to almost anything if it will calm things down; I am told I am wishy-washy and unreliable. The things that bring out the worst in me are unfriendliness, disapproval, having to work to deadlines, and being egged on to play for laughs.

(Based on 'style profiles' devised by Gilmore and Fraleigh)

5 Seeing Yourself As Part of the Problem

When I am caught up in a conflict, I see the other person as the problem. The solution is easy: she or he needs to change!

But, in almost every case, the way *I* have behaved has determined (at least to some extent) how things have panned out. If I am prepared to examine my own responses to the conflict, I may learn that I am less constructive than I had thought. Perhaps I am rolling out an unhelpful pattern of behaviour on autopilot, or I am completely misunderstanding the other person.

I find that a useful litmus test is to stop and examine how I am praying about the issue. Sometimes I am not. Why? Is God not concerned about all this? Am I afraid that he will not be very sympathetic? Sometimes my prayer boils down to, 'Lord, please prove them wrong; help me to win this one …because I'm on your side.' Are they praying that prayer too? Am I praying against powers and principalities or against people that Christ died for?

To Do When a Conflict is Escalating

You need two chairs for this. Sit in one and have the other facing you.

Concentrate on your feelings towards the person, X, who is in dispute with you. Express those feelings honestly to God in prayer. (He already knows, so you do not have to play them down.)

Pray, 'Lord, you know how grieved I feel. X has become my enemy but you have taught me to pray for my enemies.'

Now imagine X sitting in the chair opposite you. How would you explain your feelings to him or her?

Go and sit in X's chair. How does this all look from X's point of view? What would X's prayer be?

Return to your own chair and pray for God's blessing on X.

- You may find it helpful to pray *out loud*.
- Verses from the Psalms may help you to pray your feelings (try Psalms 13, 22, 52, 69, 109, 143).

As a church leader, I have a particular difficulty. I like to see myself as an objective, caring person who can help others to solve their problems, so I am slower than most to recognize when I am in fact *part* of the problem. It shakes my role. It forces me to examine how I am using my power.

Ways in Which Church Leaders Can Be Part of the Problem

Trying to Subdue Conflict by Sheer Force of Personality
This may be all right as a short-term holding measure but it ensures that the underlying causes are never addressed. Congregations subjected to this sort of leadership are never going to produce people who are active in resolving conflict themselves.

Letting Dominant People Set the Agenda
This is the opposite approach—a reluctance to use your power—but it has a similar result. Because you will not face up to powerful personalities, nobody else learns how to do so either.

Wearing Two Hats at Once
Church leaders have multiple roles, and need to be clear which role they are adopting in each circumstance. For example, a minister chairing a church business meeting cannot, in the role of pastor, argue strongly in favour of a particular proposal at the same time as being objective as a chairman.

Failing to Declare Your Intentions
Whether it is deliberate or not, keeping people in the dark creates mistrust. Much unnecessary conflict arises because of unease about where something may be leading. Good proposals can go down in flames because people felt they were being manipulated into voting for them.

Using the Pulpit for Personal Rebukes
It is very tempting to write sermons that are angled at particular people who are making life difficult for you, all the while convincing yourself, 'I am just preaching the word.' However, the unspoken words, 'And this means *you*!' will be picked up. Sermons should never be delivered as messages that apply to the hearer but not to the preacher.

Denying Your Own Anger
You may have been deeply wounded by what others have done to you, yet feel that it is wrong for a Christian leader to get angry—another role-based problem. It is possible to convince yourself that you are not angry, but you will be the only person who is fooled. Anger—whether it is cold or hot—shows in the way you treat others and just builds a wall round you.

6 Seeing Yourself As Part of the Solution

When I am caught up in conflict, I need to get beyond my initial reaction of 'This can't go on. We must sort things out…but they *will have to make the first move.'*

Putting it bluntly, if God took that attitude, he would never have been reconciled with humankind. And Christians are called to be imitators of God (Ephesians 5.1). I am tempted to say, 'How can we get anywhere when we just don't trust each other?' But underneath I am just frightened to risk the first step of building up trust…It might not work…Help!…The only person whose behaviour I can change is *me*…Yet the way I act *can* evoke a change in behaviour from others. That is how God's love works, after all, and to say otherwise is to deny the message of hope in the gospel.

So, I must be prepared to make a move. But vague exhortations from other people (such as, 'Just do it' or 'Be assertive') do not help. Personally, I need concrete suggestions for what to say or do in specific circumstances, and I prefer to practise things in front of a mirror! For some time now, I have been trying to develop three specific skills—active listening, confronting, and stating my purpose. They can be taught, and practised in role plays—although, in the end, it is the informal circumstances of real life that are the laboratory in which I develop new habits of behaviour.

Active Listening

In many cases, *confusion* is what sows the first seeds of conflict. The starting point is a misunderstanding about what others are up to. Suppose you say something to me. If I do not listen accurately, what I hear is not what you meant. Actually, I guess a lot. I interpret your behaviour by thinking to myself, 'If *I* were doing that, it would be because…' But you are not me. Your motives and feelings may be quite different from what I think they are. And if my misunderstanding provokes you, I may further misinterpret your responses, and make matters worse. After all, I would not respond like that! But by acting so as to break the cycle of confusion, I can be part of the solution to the conflict. I need to listen more carefully.

Active listening has as its goal *understanding*, not mere hearing. People in conflict tend to take each other's words *too literally*. So I practise listening tightly to the meaning but loosely to the words themselves. Then I have to check that I have really understood what I have heard by paraphrasing it back to you. I say, 'Tell me if I've got this right' and I try to be humble enough to have another go if you say I have not understood at all.

Confronting

Confronting, provided it is done early enough, will often prevent conflict from deepening. But I tend to leave it far too late. I think that is because my English church culture militates quite strongly against speaking the truth in love (Eph 4.15). We hide our feelings and we talk about people behind their backs; we would rather savour grievances than restore relationships. One might almost suppose that Jesus said, 'If someone upsets you just forget it; but, if they were *really* nasty, first complain about it to your friends, then complain about it to the minister and ask him to sort it out.' It is not that most Christians have tried following Jesus' precept (Matthew 18.15) and discovered it did not work. We have simply found the prospect frightening and not tried it. But the brave few would say that, in fact, raising a contentious issue with someone else is often less painful in reality than it is in imagination, provided it is not done judgmentally or in a burst of pent-up anger.

We would rather savour grievances than restore relationships

How Confrontation Worked

I had found my boss somewhat difficult to work with, in spite of the fact that we're both Christians. He has a tendency to fire off in all directions then get very defensive when challenged. I hate confrontation, so I have always just given up glumly when he doesn't seem to want to listen. However, I went on a training course about responding appropriately to different sorts of people. I was taught that his sort of personality needs help with listening and appreciates people who state their purpose very directly.

A few weeks later, at a staff meeting, I raised an issue which I felt needed sorting out. I stated the problem in what I thought was an exploratory sort of way. He responded with a long forceful speech in which he said that he was tired of hearing this sort of complaint. It produced a silence round the table, and we passed on to other topics. I decided not to let the matter drop, so when there was a chance, I said politely but firmly, 'John, I raised a matter earlier because I thought it needed some action from all of us and we should discuss what to do. It wasn't meant to be a criticism, but I feel that you just berated me for even mentioning it.' I was staggered by his response. Far from getting very angry, he apologised quite humbly and said it was because he had had lots of people grumbling at him in the past few days and it had made him very fed up. I understand him much better now.

If you are going to confront someone, there is a simple skill with wide application: phrasing your words as 'I messages.' This means beginning statements with *I* rather than *you*. For example, 'I think what you said at house group yesterday was unfair.' This is a truthful statement which invites further discussion. Compare: 'You are so unfair!'—a judgment on someone's character that invites a hostile response. The point of this sort of 'I message' is to make clear the impact that someone else's behaviour has had upon you. By confronting in this way, you are allowing that there may have been no deliberate slight, but you want the other person to understand why you are hurt.

'I messaging' is not especially difficult to learn or teach. The hard part is to remember to do it when you are hot under the collar, so it is a skill best practised first in situations where you can take the lead and you are not likely to get a vicious return of serve.

To Do

Here are some examples of how not to confront. Rephrase them as *impact statements*: 'I thought/felt X when you did Y.'

- 'You made me very upset. You're so rude about my catering.'
- 'You're always ramming the Bible down my throat.'
- 'You were just trying to shut me up by finishing that meeting early.'
- 'You only ever choose music that the old people like.'
- 'The trouble with you is that you don't believe the Word of God.'

Stating Your Purpose

If I confront someone, there is no guarantee that a constructive exchange will ensue. In particular, if I do not explain *why* I am doing what I am doing, others may simply guess. I can take some of the guesswork out of the dialogue by *stating my purpose*, and encouraging the other person to do the same. 'I've come to talk to you because I was very angry this morning' says in a straightforward way why I am there. (Much better than talking for 45 minutes about something else then finally broaching the subject.) When someone approaches me angrily for no apparent reason, I can say, 'Please tell me why you are raising this matter.' (Much better than, 'This seems a rather pointless fuss.')

Stating your purpose is also a way of defusing conflict at source. For example, it should be the habit of anyone chairing a meeting to say at the outset *why* it has been called and to explain the process by which decisions (if any) will be reached. Or, again, when you are dealing with someone who has a very different personality from your own, stating your purpose can prevent that person from making false assumptions about why you are behaving in a certain way. ('Oh, I thought you wanted to talk me into doing something, but actually you're just thinking out loud…')

What if None of This Works?

I have written in this chapter about approaches which, in my experience, can make a real difference. But they are not a set of tricks that are guaranteed to produce results. (If you see a book with a title like *Seven Simple Steps to Resolve Your Church's Conflict*, do not buy it.) It is possible that you have prayed carefully, you have tried to be honest about your own motives, you have been open to learning that you are part of the problem, you have listened, confronted and stated your purpose…and everything is still stuck.

When I get to this point, I have to recognize that I can only be *part* of the solution. I am not the only player. I cannot change hearts; only God can. Maybe the problem is that I see it as a *problem*. Is God more concerned with healing relationships than solving my problem? I may need to pray, 'Where is my Father working?' and discover that it is my own heart he wants to concentrate on for the moment. Maybe the only thing God wants me to learn at this point is patience—and the grace to spot the moment at which there is something new to respond to.

Or maybe I need to stop being the heroic leader who shoulders all this burden by himself. I would feel an inadequate fool if I had to call in outside help. But I know that I have had the privilege of coming alongside others in conflict. I have wished that they had seen the need for mediation earlier. Yet, even so, I have discovered that I, by being less anxious than they are, can be the catalyst for hearing one another's stories properly for the first time and taking the first step out of the bog. Can I swallow my pride and receive that sort of helping hand, as well as giving it?

7

Handling Diversity

I am convinced that, if Christians practised the things I have discussed in the previous chapters, there would be far less damaging interpersonal conflict in our churches.

But I also recognize that there is a further dimension to the problem. Conflict is sometimes a congregational (rather than simply an interpersonal) matter. Congregations can have ingrained or inherited patterns of bad behaviour. Each congregation has its house-style for responding to conflict, and Christian leaders need to help their congregations to recognize unhelpful patterns and explore how new ones can be learned. I have found that, by encouraging reflection on how Christians handle diversity and make decisions together, they can learn to respond more constructively to conflict. These issues form the subject matter for the present chapter and the following one.

The Bible affirms that diversity is part of God's creative plan. It is a plain fact that human beings come in all shapes and sizes, but their variety is given new dignity and purpose when united in the body of Christ. Members are differently gifted by the Spirit and everyone's gifts are needed by the body (Rom 12.4–5, 1 Cor 12.4–7, Eph 4.11–13). These are inspiring ideas which were in a certain sense rediscovered by the church in the 20th century. But how *subversive* they are! Affirm diversity and you provoke conflict, because for many people difference equals threat.

Diversity as a Strength

How can Christians start to see diversity as a strength? One key is to give them a taste of discovering what they already are, rather than always telling them what they *ought* to be. Let me give two examples.

In the past 20 years many Christians have got enthusiastic about exploring differences in personality. The value of such an exercise, I suggest, does not really depend on the particular scheme you use (Myers-Briggs, or whatever). What matters is affirming that each personality type has its particular strengths and weaknesses and that different types may need to work at understanding one another. However, some people are doubtful about the possible value of discovering their own type ('Won't it just be navel-gazing?')

unless they can see in advance that it might be a tool for spiritual growth. Not surprisingly, Christian experience is a more welcome starting point than secular psychology. Therefore I run workshops that show how different people encounter God in different ways. Based on a typology devised by Corinne Ware, I focus on four 'spiritual types':

A Kingdom Christian
I am a pragmatic sort of Christian. I think I am closest to God when I am making a difference to the world and I like to be a visionary leader, challenging people to obey God whatever it costs. I am keen on praying on the streets, working with people who have original ideas and knowing the signs of the times. I do not like worship that is cosy and inward-looking, armchair Christianity, or committee meetings. I am told I have a one-track mind and I should be more open to joy and dependence on God. My favourite gospel is probably Mark.

A Head Christian
I am a thinking sort of Christian. God speaks to me as I grapple with words and ideas, when I see how the Bible makes sense, and I like helping others to understand what it is all about. I am keen on well thought-out programmes, study groups and good preaching. I do not like services running on late, songs with mindless words, or political sermons. I am told I am a bit inclined to want my own way and I should be more willing to 'waste time' with God. My favourite gospel is probably Matthew.

A Mystic Christian
I am a contemplative sort of Christian. I meet God in solitude by going beyond what I can see or hear, and I like to be a calm source of inspiration to others. I am keen on retreats, using poetry and symbols in prayer, and special friends who help my faith to grow. I do not like busy services, being talked at by Christians with bees in their bonnets, or enforced jolliness. I am told I should spend more time looking outwards and getting into discussion about my faith. My favourite gospel is probably John.

A Heart Christian
I am an affectionate sort of Christian. God's love feels very real in my heart and I like to chat to others about what he has done for me and how he has the power to change lives. I am keen on enthusiastic worship, inspiring personal testimonies, warm fellowship and extempore prayer. I do not like formal services, pointless silences, or standing still (physically or spiritually). I am told I will never admit to being angry or disappointed and I should find some out-of-church interests. My favourite gospel is probably Luke.

To Do With a Group

Think by yourselves about the question, 'What would I do if I wanted to come close to God?' (Read your Bible? Meet up with other Christians? Go for a walk? Decide what is best for you.)

Share your answers in groups of three.

Again by yourselves, read the profiles on the previous page. Each of you decide which of the four is most like you. (You may well be something of a mixture, but most people lean one way more than another.)

Now split into four groups, one for each sort of Christian. In each group:

- Share personal examples of what has helped your faith to grow.
- Put together a short sketch (fun, not heavy!) that shows how people like you get frustrated with church life.

Then each group present its sketch to the others.

Finally, reflect together: What have we learned about each other? About our church? About God?

I also run workshops on the intensely practical topic *Communicating Under Pressure*. They help people to be alert to several styles of communication (and, in some cases, to understand a spouse for the first time!). These workshops are based on the four types ('colours') described on page 11. As with the four 'spiritual types' on page 19, the scheme is simple enough to avoid the workshop getting too technical.

I hope it is clear that workshops like these can develop people's resources for facing church conflict. For many a Christian, doing a 'spiritual type' workshop feels like finally being give permission to be the person God has made you to be. (One comment: 'That was a liberating experience.') When you are more confident that you are loved by God and made in a certain way, you are less likely to feel threatened by others who are different. You start to appreciate the strengths that they offer to the Body as a whole.

Gospel and Culture

Congregations often have a strong line on cultural norms and who is allowed to set them. In other words, what you get is what the powerful people like. Granted, reasoned arguments are presented for why things should be done in a certain way but I am convinced that much of what masquerades as doctrinal principle is in fact a matter of personal preference. We are all liable to pay more attention to human traditions than to the commands of God (Mk 7.8)—even if those traditions are only 10 years old. But the price is high. In such a culture, challenge is unacceptable, so constructive ways through conflict are never explored.

There is a different way. I have never forgotten hearing Festo Kivengere, an African bishop, urging an audience of British Christians to take Romans 14 seriously. Here was a man from an entirely different culture saying, in the 1970s, 'Do not let culture divide us.' 'Let us be clear,' he added, 'that we cannot compromise the gospel. Christ died for our sins and was raised from the dead. But most issues dividing Christians are not gospel issues.' Amen! I would paraphrase Romans 14 thus: 'Stop trying to make absolute rulings on this, that or the other practice; rather, consider what is helpful to your fellow believer.' This is a mandate for a church that is, in the right sense, permission-giving rather than permission-withholding. At this point, I think, society at large is ahead of the church. For in almost every walk of life, cultural variety is encountered and is seen to be valuable. Thus we live in a world where churchy cultural ghettos are no longer credible.

Permission to Speak

Christian leaders tend to be jittery when contrary views are expressed. Understandably, we want to maintain unity. But somehow the more we try to prevent certain things from being said, the more those things get said anyway, and often in damaging ways—out of the side of the mouth, out of the minister's hearing, in the maverick house group, in the car park. I suggest that, paradoxically, being open about our differences makes destructive conflict less likely. A good personal motto is *Wherever you differ from me, I have something to learn*. And as a leader I need to be first to adopt it.

> Our vicar planned an evening to address issues of human sexuality. I thought it was very well handled. First he gave a carefully thought-out talk. It gave a clear lead but there was no sense of 'You've just got to agree with me. Full stop.' Then he gave an open invitation for others to speak, one after another. Many did so, and the vicar waited until the end before saying anything further—he just responded briefly to the points that had been raised. I was surprised at the range of views expressed. Someone said that it was one of the most helpful meetings he'd ever been to.

8 Making Decisions

The business of responding to conflict is at its sharpest when it comes to making decisions.

Some of the church meetings I have attended make 'The Holy Spirit said' (Acts 13.2) seem like a bad joke. Yet in the face of regular acrimony, how often do we stop to ask, 'Why is this happening?' My guess is that most churches have never consciously reflected upon how they make decisions, nor considered whether there might be alternative approaches.

Some Common Complaints

Presumed consensus ('I never got the chance to say I disagree.')
Foregone conclusions ('We all know "They" have already decided…')
Hidden agendas ('I wonder if those are the real reasons?')
Stalling ('When are we going to get the chance to discuss this properly?')
Racing ('We were rushed into giving a verdict before we had time to think.')
Rigging ('That way of voting could only produce one result.')

Think for a moment about some occasion when a church decision made you angry. What was the problem? They decided to do something fundamentally unChristian? Probably not. In my experience, anger often stems from disquiet with the *way* in which a decision was reached, rather than from the content of the decision itself. This suggests that a key to making better decisions is to give more attention to the *process*.

Leaders can profitably ask:

- What are we doing to help everyone speak the truth in love?
- What are we doing to promote real understanding of the issues?
- How are we attending to the voice of the Holy Spirit?

An Exercise for a Church Council

- 'Everybody knows what the Council is *for*.'
- 'Silent people understand what is going on.'
- 'If nobody disagrees, it means everybody agrees.'

Which of these statements is true of our Council?
Talk about your impressions, in pairs, then in the whole Council.

The way that decisions are made should say that people matter. Not that they should always get what they want, but certainly that they are not simply being sacrificed on the altar of Project or Principle. The person who disagrees may be a thorn in the flesh but he or she is entitled to the same courtesy as anyone else—and may have a prophetic insight to offer.

I am surprised how often Christians seem to think it is not even worth having a go at seeking consensus. I do not mean *unanimity*. I mean an appropriate level of consent—which might be anything from full support to 'We will live with this without undermining it.'

In Zimbabwe, *runyararo* is a traditional custom. When two parties cannot reach agreement in discussion, one may eventually declare *runyararo*. It is a powerful symbolic gesture that means 'for the good of the tribe, I will go along with what the other party wants.' I think we are the poorer for having no similar ritual in our own culture.

Finding consensus takes longer than 'like it or lump it' but surely it cannot be right for churches to make major decisions that leave most members feeling nobody even wanted to hear their opinion or tell them what was going on. We should not behave as if the Holy Spirit only ever speaks through a few key people in the congregation.

I would say that our whole way of running meetings gives undue influence to articulate, confident or domineering individuals. Usually we offer people only two ways of expressing their opinions: (a) speaking in open debate, and (b) voting yes or no. But if you are nervous, or stumble over your words, dare you respond to a polished or aggressive speech? Perhaps you wait to see how others vote before you raise your hand. I think churches should make more effort to ensure that everyone is listened to. There are better ways of helping people to register their views, approaches that encourage the quiet (but not necessarily unwise) majority.

A Checklist for Decisions

- Who should make the decision?
- Who should be consulted?
- Is the decision far-reaching?
- If so, have we allowed enough time for reflection and prayer?
- Is consensus important?
- If so, how will it be tested?
- Has the procedure been explained?
- Who needs to know the final decision?
- How will we tell them?

Some Ways of Encouraging Better Listening

Breakout Groups

When a group larger than 5 or 6 has a proposal to discuss, split into small groups to begin with, then report back ideas from each group in the whole assembly. This allows a lot of people's ideas to be aired quickly. Keep all the groups in the same room as they talk, and you get a nice sense of 'hum.'

'Human Rainbow'

Invite the group to stand in an arc, each person taking up a position that indicates where she or he stands on a spectrum of opinion. For example, when a proposal is being considered, those strongly in favour stand at one end, those strongly against at the other, and others at appropriate positions in between. This is a very useful exercise at the halfway point towards making a decision. It is not a formal vote and it can be introduced by saying that nobody is committing him/herself to a final position yet. Nevertheless, it allows opinions of those who have not spoken up to become visible, and they will often respond readily if invited to explain why they have stood in their chosen spots.

This is a very useful exercise at the halfway point towards making a decision

Circle Sharing

Sit everyone in a circle, and ask each person in turn to say what he or she thinks or feels about the matter in hand. This ensures that everyone is heard and can make eye-contact with others while speaking. It is a good thing to do before proceeding to a formal vote on a far-reaching proposal. For example, if lots of people say they are not very sure, it would be better to postpone a final vote until there has been more time for deliberation.

'Samoan Circle'

Set out most of the chairs in a circle, but put three or four in a smaller inner circle. Adopt the convention that only people in the inner circle may speak; those in the outer circle simply listen. Anyone in the outer circle who wishes to speak may go and join the discussion in the centre. If there is no empty chair, the new arrival stands behind the chair of someone who has already had a fair turn; that person must quickly vacate the chair. This procedure works well to change the dynamic of a large group in which several people tend to talk at once and do not listen to each other.

This works well to change the dynamic of a large group in which several people tend to talk at once

Mapping Progress
Use a board or flip chart that everyone can see. Ask one person in the group to note up important points as they are made. Stop at intervals and invite the group to review progress, summarize conclusions so far, and possibly even celebrate achievement. This is a much more productive procedure than having minutes that nobody sees until after the meeting. The work of the group becomes something visible at a time when it can help to dispel confusion.

Pausing for Prayer
Call for a period of prayer to allow for listening to God. This can happen during the course of a meeting or between meetings. If there is conflict in the air, it is appropriate to acknowledge it before God, and to seek love and wisdom from the Holy Spirit. A short time of silent prayer can provide a most important break in the flow of words.

Focussing on the Process

When you try out any of these approaches for the first time, remember to explain *why* you want to do it (purpose-stating to the fore again). Emphasize that establishing a culture of learning through conflict requires more reflection and less talk when making decisions.

Encourage decision-making groups to reflect upon the process *as they go along*. They learn thereby to attend to *relationships* as well as *issues*. For example, it can be very helpful to elicit comments on any change in mood or any development in consensus. Doing so encourages people to recognize how their behaviour is—or is not—transforming conflict.

Encouraging Reflection on the Process of a Meeting

'How have your feelings about this proposal altered during the past hour?'

'I think we're much closer to agreement than we were. How do others see it?'

'We seem to have got very heated about this. Why do you think that has happened?'

'Do we need to take a break?'

'Tell me why we've had a long silence.'

'What do you think we've learned by doing it this way?'

9 Putting It All Together

After the twin towers came down on 11th September 2001, the world had an unparalleled opportunity to hear how Americans were responding.

I was listening to reporters from all over the world interviewing distressed people. At first, the responses were concerned with how to improve defences. ('We will make sure they can never do this to us again.') Soon they moved onto taking control of world events. ('We will engage in a war against terror.') Then I heard one man saying, 'I'm starting to ask "Why do they *hate* us so much?"' At that point I felt there was hope of a better way.

Learning through conflict means going beyond being defensiv and beyond trying to assert control

Churches in conflict will produce the same initial reactions. Defence—we do what will immediately stop us feeling hurt. Control—we use what power we have to keep others in check. Both of these are understandable and sometimes even necessary. But I have been saying in this booklet that learning through conflict means going beyond being defensive and beyond trying to assert control. It means asking *why* things are happening this way. Not just 'How can we cope?' but also 'What is God trying to teach us?'

I hope I have challenged you to ask yourself, 'How can I help to build congregations that are made stronger through inevitable conflict rather than being torn apart by it?'

Questions for You

- How do I normally respond to conflict?
- Do I talk *to* people or *about* them?

In any current conflict:

- How I am a part of the problem?
- How can I be part of the solution?
- Am I trying to play God?

Questions for Your Church's Leadership Team

- How does our church handle diversity?
- How do we make decisions?
- What destructive habits do we have as a congregation?
- In what situations do they become apparent?
- What constructive habits could we start modelling?

A Better Metaphor

On page 7, I suggested that we need a better image for church conflict than stones tumbling in a polisher. What metaphor would *you* choose?

Mine is illustrated on the front cover. Being in conflict is like having a chisel put in my hand. I have the power to inflict considerable damage on others. But by asking myself, 'What can we *learn* here?' I can find the wisdom to use the chisel differently. By confronting the person who has wronged me, but also by listening, repenting and forgiving, I can help us both to be formed further into the image of Christ.

Your Action Plan

Note here any specific things you intend to do as a result of reading this booklet:

10 Further Resources

Carolyn Schrock-Shenk and Lawrence Ressler (eds), *Making Peace With Conflict* (Herald Press, 1999, ISBN 0836191277). Fleshes out a lot of what you have read in the present booklet.

Yvonne Joan Craig, *Peacemaking for Churches* (SPCK, 1999, ISBN 0281051771). A guide to biblical principles and practical approaches for mediation.

Carolyn Schrock-Shenk (ed), *Mediation and Facilitation Training Manual: Foundations and Skills for Constructive Conflict Transformation, 4th ed* (Mennonite Conciliation Service, 2000, ISBN 0964200309). A goldmine of short articles. Lots of practical exercises. Especially good on working with groups.

Susan Gilmore and Patrick Fraleigh, *Style Profile for Communication at Work* (Friendly Press, 1992, ISBN 0938070118). A guide to understanding the way you communicate with others and how it changes when you are under pressure.

David Augsburger, *Caring Enough to Confront, 2nd ed* (Herald Press, 1980, ISBN 0836119282). Excellent on finding the right way of saying things.

Corinne Ware, *Discover Your Spiritual Type* (The Alban Institute, 1995, ISBN 1566991498). A guide to different pathways of growth for different Christians.

Richard Foster, *Streams of Living Water: Celebrating the Great Traditions of Christian Faith* (Harper Collins, 1998, ISBN 0006281303). An inspiring study of how different Christian traditions are beginning to learn from one another.

James Bryan Smith, *Spiritual Formation Workbook* (HarperCollins Fount, 1999, ISBN 0006281478). A companion to Foster's book. Useful for small groups.

Alastair McKay, *Decision Making for Churches (Adminisheet No 58)* (Administry, 1997). Much good advice packed into 2 sides of A4.

Bridge Builders (www.menno.org.uk/BB/) offers training in skills for transforming church conflicts, and co-ordinates a national network of mediators.